THE GOLDEN THREAD

BLUECOAT

Published by Bluecoat Press, Liverpool.
(c) All the photographs are the copyright of
Patrick Ward, except his selected essay from
the Port of London archive.
Artwork by Daniel Bickerton.
Printed in Slovenia by Latitude Press.

*"The Thames is no ordinary waterway, it is
the golden thread of our nation's history"*

Sir Winston Churchill

THE GOLDEN THREAD

The River Thames from Source to Sea

Patrick Ward

Foreword

The River Thames is many things to many people. A transport artery for passengers and freight. A place to row, sail or to walk. An essential part of London's rich heritage and home to an increasingly robust economy.

At the Port pf London Authority it is our great privilege to be Custodians of the Tidal Thames, which runs 95 miles from Teddington in West London through the capital, to the heart of the commercial port and on out to the North Sea.

This great river is treasured as a place of beauty and majesty, bringing pleasure to millions of people on its waters, on its bridges and its banks, or looking down from the many buildings that now grace its path.

We are proud to support the publication of this book and to give more people a chance to enjoy at their leisure the many attractions both on and surrounding the river.

We hope this book will inspire you to visit the Thames and to spend time, either at work or at play, enjoying one of our nation's most iconic assets.

Christopher Rodrigues CBE
Port of London Authority Chairman

The Working Thames

This book is largely about the River Thames at play but there was once another Thames, a river devoted to hard labour in its vast dockyards, where the imports and exports of a still great Empire were manhandled by an army of dockers. These images, drawn from the archives of the Port of London Authority, give us a moving record of those days and of the men of character, stoicism and humour who lived and worked there.

1880. Directors of Morgan and Lang, above, pose proudly before newly completed works at Surrey Commercial Dock

1900. South West India Docks, right, with a forest of Thames sailing barges and lightermen rowing in mid-dock

Thank you Port of London Authority for your generous
support and for opening up your archives for this essay

9

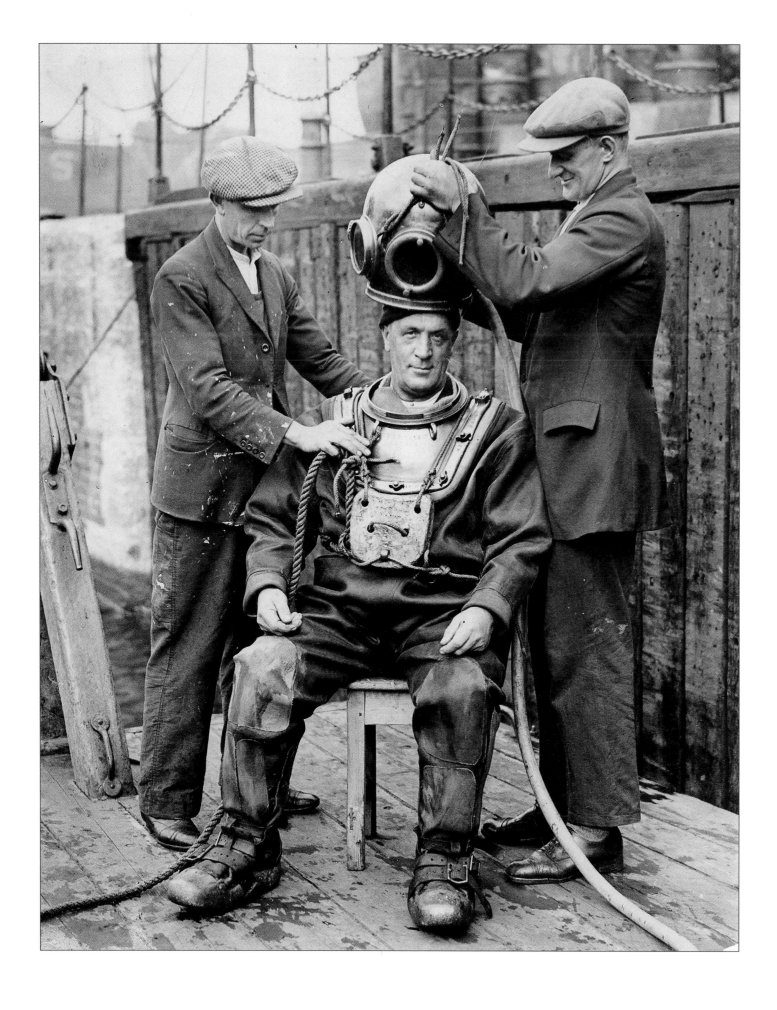

1930. The Port of London Authority's steam dredger Number 10 working with a support tug in the Thames estuary

1930. A PLA diver, preparing for wreck raising work, often in such murky waters that his touch has to replace his sight

1944. General Montgomery addresses 16,000 port workers before the invasion of France

1940. Four years earlier firefighters struggle to save Thameside warehouses during the Blitz

1920. Dockers with barrows haul away bags of beet sugar from a coasting vessel at West Dock

1942. The PLA's Mobile Canteen No. 2 brews tea for the dockers, much valued for their contribution to the war effort during this time

1930 Prime Minister Ramsay MacDonald moors the first ship to arrive at Tilbury's new passenger landing stage

1921 Opening of the King George V Dock, right, a special day for the Port of London Authority

1949 A Morris car being craned aboard a ship en route to its new owner in Singapore

1945 Dust covered dockers load Canadian flour onto an electric vehicle

1920s Limehouse Reach with a coaster following a Thames steam tug, once used widely along the tidal reaches of the Thames

1930. Not the Keystone Cops but the Port of London Authority's very own police force, test life jackets the hard way at West India Dock

Jerome K. Jerome

In 1888 Jerome Klapka Jerome married Elizabeth Henrietta Marris and, to our great good fortune they spent their honeymoon aboard a small boat on the River Thames. On their return Jerome, then aged 29, sat down and wrote his masterpiece, "Three Men in a Boat". In the novel Elizabeth, his "Ellie", was transformed into two longtime male friends, George and Harris. This device enabled Jerome to create comic and sometimes moving situations around an imaginary boating trip with them from Kingston to Oxford.

The book was published in 1889 and became an immediate success and remains in print to this day. Its popularity was such that the number of boats registered on the Thames increased by fifty percent in the year following its publication and it contributed greatly to the popularity of the Thames as a tourist attraction. The book sold over a million copies during the following 25 years and allowed Jerome, who had previously tried an acting career, to become a full-time author. Some years later he wrote "Three Men on the Bummel". This had the same three characters making a cycling tour in Germany but, sadly, this project was not so successful as it lacked the life-force and insights of his first great book on the River Thames.

I so enjoyed "Three Men in a Boat", with its warmth, quirky humour and occasional pathos, that I have chosen short passages from it to run through this book. Hopefully, I've also chosen adjoining photographs which I hope are in sympathy with the great man's words. If you enjoy these short excerpts do please read the original book. Although written over a century ago, it still feels as funny, alive and relevant as when he first sat down to write it, inspired by his honeymoon trip up the Thames with his new bride, dear "Ellie".

Photographer's Notes

It's mid-November and I'm on my houseboat, which is straining at its moorings just half a mile up-river from Hampton Court Palace. Outside my windows the normally calm River Thames, now brown and angry, is surging past. Ducks and geese, trying to cross from bank to bank, are swept helplessly past in the racing tide. At this moment it would be easy to agree with T.S. Eliot who wrote, "I do not know much about gods, but I think that the river is a strong brown god". Still he also wrote, perhaps on a calmer day, "The river is within us". Having lived on the Thames for the past 25 years and experienced it in all its moods I'm inclined to share both of these sentiments.

The Thames is not a great river if size and length are the criteria, for it flows a mere 215 miles from its modest source in a Cotswolds meadow to the open sea some 30 miles east of London. But then how does one measure the stature of a river that glides serenely through such historic communities as Abingdon, Oxford, Henley, Eton, Hampton Court, Westminster, the City of London and Greenwich? Winston Churchill gave a typically robust answer when he declared, "The Thames is no ordinary waterway, it is the golden thread of our nation's history".

Perhaps a major reason for the river's continuing and indeed growing appeal is that all but 25 miles of its length is navigable, something we Thames lovers take full advantage of. From my vantage point here at Hampton, I'm tempted to believe that summers last for seven or eight months, because from Easter until well into October the river is a busy highway carrying craft of every shape and size up and down its length. The action commences at sunrise with rowing eights and their megaphone-toting umpire launches racing by on their training sessions, creating enough turbulence to set my solid double decker home rocking on its moorings. So much for lie-ins then!

Then come the narrowboats, crewed by the true gentry of the Thames, with their characteristic single-cylinder engines easing them along at a sedate pace, at one with both their surroundings and the wildlife. Later in the day grand plastic motor yachts emerge from their exclusive marinas, their owners and guests often seeming as overweight as their floating gin palaces. But even they are upstaged by the converted Dutch barges such as "Magna Carta", a floating hotel much loved by American tourists, which majestically cruise along the Thames. However, these cleverly designed vessels, with their collapsible wheel houses, can pass beneath the low bridges spanning the Thames further up-river, where more extravagant motor launches, with their flying bridges, can no longer venture. By sunset, the lock keepers have gone home and river traffic has dwindled, the perfect time for this Thames lover to head out for an evening paddle in his kayak.

Meanwhile, on the riverbank opposite my home a different day unfolds. This is where the Thames Path, which runs virtually the whole length of the river, passes by. The morning starts with a flurry of dog walkers, doing their duty whatever the weather. They are followed by the cyclists, rushing to work during the week, or pedalling on charity runs at the weekend. Later in the day, the bench directly opposite my houseboat becomes the meeting point for anglers, bird feeding families, pensive old boys and, occasionally, young lovers too.

So why is the Thames so special ? Well, I think it casts a spell on all who spend time on its banks and upon its waters. Its gentle pace and serenity, well maybe not in November, slows us down and gives us time to relax and contemplate and to feel part of something bigger than ourselves, a kind of life force. People seem kinder and gentler on the river. In 25 years afloat I've only once witnessed an angry shouting match, and that soon became a pantomime performance, unable to survive the river's calming influence.

The photographs that follow aim to capture the special relationship between the river and the English who love and enjoy it, because the spell of the Thames is such that we all perhaps become honorary English men and women when we stroll along her banks or float upon her waters. Visit the Royal Henley Regatta or, better still, the lesser known events further up river, or spend a day following the historic annual Swan Upping ceremony, or cadge a ride at the Electric Boat Rally and glide silently among the swans, and I think you might just agree. But don't buy a houseboat, because then you might never leaver great river.

Patrick Ward,
Taggs Island, 2018

Helmsley.
A modest stone in a Cotswold meadow marks the claimed source of the River Thames

From Source to Sea, the Journey Begins

Cricklade. Flowing past this small Cotswold community the Thames is still just a meandering stream

Cricklade. **Ponies graze on a Thames that is yet to come to life**

Lechlade. An angler enjoys his fishing below Lechlade, where only the occasional narrowboat intrudes.

Lechlade. Small craft, like this narrowboat, are able to venture up-river to this narrow and peaceful stretch of the Thames

Buscot. Afternoon tea aboard the Edwardian steam launch "Churr", built by the Lune Valley Company in 1910

Lechlade. Swans beneath Halfpenny Bridge and nesting nearby.
A halfpenny was the toll paid by pedestrians to cross the Thames here until 1839

Old ladies, not accustomed to the river, are always intensely nervous

of steam launches. I remember going up once from Staines to

Windsor - a stretch of water peculiarly rich in these mechanical

monstrosities - with a party containing three ladies of this description.

It was very exciting.

At the first glimpse of every steam-launch that came into view,

they insisted on landing and sitting down on the bank until it was

out of sight again. They said they were very sorry, but that they

owed it to their families not to be foolhardy.

Jerome K. Jerome, Three Men in a Boat

Kelmscott.
**People and their dogs socialise at
the Plough Inn's riverside garden**

Newbridge. The wonderfully named pub, the Rose Revived, overlooks the New Bridge, built in the thirteenth century and one of the first bridges to span the River Thames

Radcot. The bridge in this small village, though much restored, claims to be even older than the one at Newbridge

Oxford. Punting and posing beneath Magdalen Bridge, on a tributary of the Thames, the River Cherwell

Oxford. Moment of contact, above, during the Oxford University Bump Races on the Isis, a re-named section of the Thames flowing through the city. The river here is too narrow for skiffs to race side by side - hence the "bumps" instead

Oxford to Abingdon. Cruising on a summer tourist boat between these two towns

Oxford to Abingdon. A boathouse, perhaps now a riverside home, and a narrowboat moored near Abingdon

If you stay the night at Clifton, you cannot do better than put up

at the "Barley Mow". It is without exception, I would say, the quaintest,

most old world inn up the river. It stands on the right of the bridge, quite

away from the village. Its low pitched gables and thatched roof and

latticed windows give it quite a story-book appearance, while inside

it is even still more once-upon-a-timeyfied.

It would not be a good place for the heroine of a modern novel to stay at.

The heroine of a modern novel is always "divinely tall" and she is ever

"drawing herself up to her full height". At the "Barley Mow" she would

bang her head against the ceiling each time she did this.

Jerome K. Jerome, Three Men in a Boat

Abingdon.
The town has hosted a Benedictine
monastery since the seventh century and
has held a Monday market since 1556

Wallingford.
The annual Raft Races are held beneath the town bridge and raise funds for local charities.

Wallingford.
Teams build their own rafts for the races, some with mixed success

Pangbourne. The restored steam launch "Alaska" catches the evening light at Goring Gap, at the end of the annual narrowboat rally

Near Marlow.
Swan Uppers get a welcome tow from the steam launch "Eclipse", as they head up-river during their traditional five day annual event

Near Hurley Members of the Dyers and Vintners companies capture the Queen's swans, to be weighed and marked during the annual Swan Upping event

Near Hurley An angry swan protects her cygnets from the Swan Uppers, who always treat them with great care

Girls too don't look half bad in a boat, if prettily dressed.

Nothing is more fetching, to my way of thinking, than a

tasteful boating costume. But a "boating costume", it

would be as well if all ladies would understand, ought

to be a costume that can be worn on a boat, and not

merely under a glass case. It utterly spoils an excursion

if you have folk in the boat who are thinking all the time

a good deal more of their dress than of the trip. It was my

misfortune to go for a water picnic with two ladies of this

kind. We did have a lively time!

Jerome K. Jerome, Three Men in a Boat

Sonning. The skipper of the tourist launch African Queen ducks as he guides her beneath the low arches of Sonning Bridge

Henley.
The steam launch "Sabrina", built
in 1870, lowers her funnel to pass
beneath Henley Bridge during a
traditional boat rally

Shiplake. The electric canoe "Pippa" glides silently up the course at the Shiplake and Wargrave Regatta, complete with wine and food hamper

Shiplake. **This regatta is a relaxed family affair, with the Greasy Pole Competition taking pride of place on the final evening**

Shiplake. The Thameside communities of Shiplake and Margrave face each other across the river, so there is much ferrying back and forth of families and children during their shared regatta

Throw the lumber over man! Let your boat of life be light,

packed only with what you need - a homely home and simple

pleasures, one or two friends, worth the name, someone to

love and someone to love you, a cat, a dog, and a pipe or

two, enough to drink; for thirst is a dangerous thing.

You will find the boat easier to pull then, and it will not be so

liable to upset; good plain merchandise will stand water.

You will have time to think as well as to work. Time to drink in life's

sunshine - time to listen to the Aeolian music that the wind of

God draws from the human heartstrings around us.

Jerome K. Jerome, Three Men in a Boat

Henley. A view of the course for the Henley Royal Regatta, the annual sporting and social highlight of life on the River Thames. The competitors, above, are checking the day's rowing programme in the very dress conscious Stewards Enclosure

Henley. The race begins, with a mile and 550 yards to the finish for crews who come from schools and universities worldwide to compete in the Henley Royal Regatta

Henley. Umpires following each race firmly keep the rowers on their Berks and Bucks stations, named for the two counties adjoining this stretch of the river

Henley. **The moment for glory or despair at the climax of another race at Henley**

Henley.
Shoes off for a romantic interlude on the Thames towpath, but where is the owner of the third hat?

Henley.
**Chivalry lives on in the Stewards
Enclosure as the Henley Royal
Regatta comes to a muddy end**

Henley. Surviving the lunchtime rain at the Henley Royal Regatta

It's a good plan, too, if you are in a great hurry, to talk

very loudly to each other about how you don't need any

tea, and are not going to have any. You get near the kettle,

so that it can overhear you, and then you shout out, "I

don't want any tea, do you George?", to which George

shouts back, "Oh no, I don't like tea: we'll have lemonade

instead - tea's so indigestible". Upon which the kettle boils

over, and puts the stove out.

Jerome K. Jerome, Three Men in a Boat

Henley. Occurring some weeks later, Henley's more modest Town Regatta is a less grand event, though still as demanding for rowers. The umpires, this one with his teddy bear, seem a more relaxed group

Henley. Polishing the prizewinners' cups at the Henley Town Regatta and congratulations for a winning crew

Henley.
The Steam launch "Consulta" was first built for umpiring duties in 1898 but is seen here still going strong at the Henley Town Regatta some 120 years later

Henley. Guests stroll through the sculpture park at the Henley Festival of the Arts, which offers five evenings of concerts from its floating stage, as well as theatrical acts such as the French art troupe, above

Henley.
Strange meetings on the Thames towpath during the annual arts festival

Henley. **This headless couple were part of the riverside show at Henley Festival of the Arts**

I did get to sleep for a few hours, and then some part of the boat which seemed to have grown up in the night - for it was certainly not there when we started, and it had disappeared by the morning - kept digging into my spine. I slept through it for a while, dreaming that I had swallowed a sovereign, and that they were cutting a hole in my back with a gimlet, so as to try and get it out. I thought it very unkind of them, and I told them I would owe them the money, and they should have it at the end of the month. But they would not hear of that, and said it would be much better if they had it then, because otherwise the interest would accumulate, so I got quite cross with them after a bit, and told them what I thought of them, and then they gave the gimlet such an excruciating wrench that I woke up.

Jerome K. Jerome, Three Men in a Boat

Henley. **Champagne on the Thames towpath during the annual music festival**

Henley. Wining and dining on a Thames slipper launch before the concerts begin

Remenham. Bride and groom board an umpire's launch for the short journey to their wedding reception in Henley

Henley. Another bride and groom pose for their photographer on a footbridge in Henley

Henley. A fleeting kiss at the Thames Traditional Boat Festival, an annual gathering for all who love wooden boats

Henley. Travelling in style in the Chairman's craft at the Thames Traditional Boat Festival

Henley. Eccentrics are always welcome at the Traditional Boat Festival providing their boats are of wooden construction.
This delightful couple, with their steam-powered paddle boat, are sailing just within the rules

Henley. The steam launch "Sunbeam" parades along the course of the Thames Traditional Boat Festival

And a little further still, nestling by a sweet corner of the stream, is what is left of Medmenham Abbey. The famous Medmenham monks, or "Hell Fire Club", as they were commonly called, and of whom the notorious Wilkes was a member, were a fraternity whose motto was "Do as you please", and that invitation still stands over the ruined doorway of the abbey. Many years before this bogus abbey, with its congregation of irreverent jesters, was founded, there stood upon this spot a monastery of a sterner kind, whose monks were of a somewhat different type to the revellers that were to follow them, five hundred years afterwards.

Jerome K. Jerome, Three Men in a Boat

Hambledon. Riverside bliss with cottages, Thames slipper launches, a narrowboat and swans gliding by

Hambledon. **Kayakers ride the Weir beneath Hambledon Mill**

Hurley. This village stages the last of the summer regattas, noted for its lively Tug of War competitions

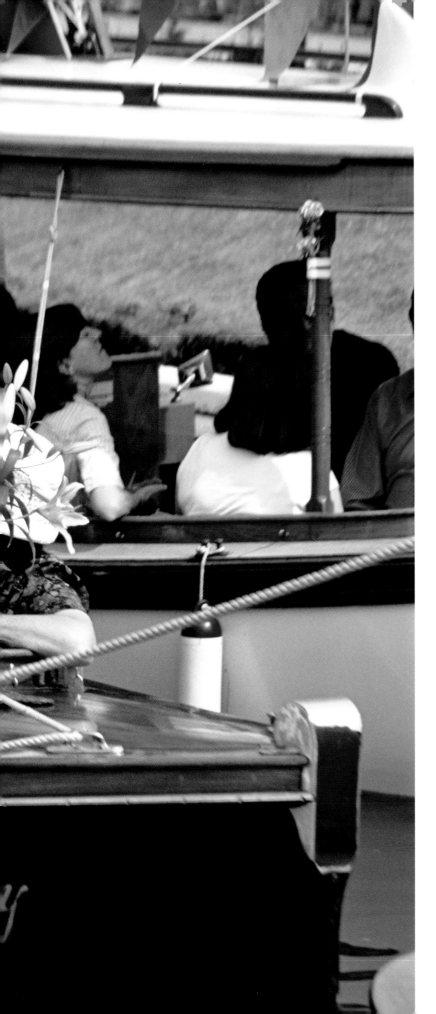

Bisham. The launch "Lilly Langtry", seen passing through Bisham Lock during the Electric Boat Association's rally, is named after the actress who was the mistress of the Prince of Wales in the 1870s

Marlow. The Chiltern Hills rise above the Thames and its pleasure boats on this stretch of the river

Marlow. One man and his dog, devoted spectators during the Dragon Boat races at the Marlow Regatta

So, eventually, he made one final arrangement with himself, which he has religiously held to ever since, and that was to count each fish he caught as ten, and to assume ten to begin with. For example, if he did not catch any fish at all, then he said he had caught ten fish - you could never catch less than ten fish by his system; that was the foundation of it. Then, if by any chance he did catch one fish, he called it twenty, while two fish would count thirty, three forty, and so on.

It is a simple and easily worked plan, and there has been some talk lately of it being made use of by the angling fraternity in general. Indeed the Committee of the Thames Angler's Association did recommend its adoption about two years ago, but some of the older members opposed it. They said they would consider the idea if the number were doubled, and if each fish counted as twenty.

Jerome K. Jerome, Three Men in a Boat

Marlow. During rare heatwave conditions these swans seemed to queue patiently at the weir of Marlow Lock to cool down

Bourne End. Meanwhile, a few miles downstream, these cows chose group meditation in the river

Cookham. Dressing the part for the Cookham Regatta while punters, at right, tackle a stiff breeze

Cliveden. Perched high above the Thames near Cookham, Cliveden was once home to the Astor family and is now owned by the National Trust. The artist, above, was painting on one of the small islands dotted along the river below the estate

Maidenhead. Kayaking enthusiasts gather to challenge the weir during the Boulters Lock Rodeo

Maidenhead. The kayaker's talent lies in getting close into the weir's raging torrent, performing set manoeuvres, and getting out again in one piece

Maidenhead. Tense competitors await the start of their race during the Thames Punting Club event, while their umpire and his pilot, right, stand by

Maidenhead itself is too snobby to be pleasant. It is the haunt

of the river swell and his overdressed female companion. It is

the town of showy hotels, patronised chiefly by dudes and

ballet girls. It is the witch's kitchen from which go forth those

demons of the river - steam launches. The London Journal duke

always has his "little place" at Maidenhead; and the heroine of

the three volume novel always dines there when she goes out on

the spree with somebody else's husband.

Jerome K. Jerome, Three Men in a Boat

Bray.
An early morning rower glides past
the village of Bray, site of some of the
grandest homes on the River Thames

Windsor.
The Oakley Court is a favourite
venue for Thameside weddings
and parties

Bray. Guests depart from the Waterside Inn, the Roux Brothers' celebrated restaurant

Near Bray. The steam launch "Eclipse" makes her leisurely way home to Shepperton,
after attending the Traditional Boat Festival at Henley

Windsor. At 6 a.m. on a Sunday morning several hundred swimmers
battle in the river beneath Windsor Castle during the town's annual triathlon competition

Eton. Disaster faced with good humour by one Eton schoolboy during the fourth of June celebrations

Eton. Carefully standing up in a narrow skiff to salute Eton, Queen and Country is the moment of truth for these Eton boys. Running the country later in life must seem a doddle.

Old Windsor.
The royal barge "Gloriana" and her supporting flotilla celebrate the 800th anniversary of the sealing of Magna Carta by King John. The barge was a gift to the Queen in 2012, to mark her Diamond Jubilee

Staines. A Sunday morning race for the Staines Sailing Club, while new life explores the river rather more sedately, above

Caesar, of course, had a little place at Walton - a camp, or an entrenchment, or something of that sort. Caesar was a regular up-river man. Also Queen Elizabeth, she was there too. You can never get away from that woman, go where you will. Cromwell and Bradshaw (not the guide man, but the King Charles's head man) likewise sojourned here. They must have been quite a pleasant little party, altogether.

There is an iron "scold's bridle" in Walton Church. They used these things in ancient times for curbing women's tongues. They have given up the attempt now. I suppose iron was getting scarce, and nothing else would be strong enough.

Jerome K. Jerome, Three Men in a Boat

Walton. An amphibious vehicle comes ashore after taking part in a river parade of military vehicles

NELSON IN DE NILE F1

Shepperton.
**Lord Nelson turns a
blind eye during the
town's annual regatta**

143

Hampton. A newly-built houseboat is towed towards its new moorings on Taggs Island

Hampton. Spring-cleaning for a houseboat owner on Taggs Island, home to a community of a hundred happily floating folk

Hampton. **May Day celebrations, right, at Garrick Temple, built by the 18th century actor David Garrick to celebrate the genius of William Shakespeare**

Hampton. Tourists cruising up-river on the "Yarmouth Belle", from its base in Kingston towards Sunbury

Hampton. **The Thames is not ideal for swimming but almost irresistible on a hot summer afternoon**

Hampton. **Water off a duck's back maybe, but more challenging for these girls getting soaked while training near Hampton Rowing Club**

For myself, I am fond of locks. They pleasantly break the monotony of the pull. I like sitting in the boat and slowly rising out of the cool depths up into new reaches and fresh views; or sinking down, as it were, out of the world, and then waiting, while the gloomy gates creak, and the narrow strip of day-light between them widens till the fair smiling river lies full before you, and you push your little boat out from its brief prison on to the welcoming waters once again.

They are picturesque little spots, these locks. The stout old lock-keeper, or his cheerful-looking wife, or bright-eyed daughter, are pleasant folk to have a passing chat with. You meet other boats there, and river gossip is exchanged. The Thames would not be the fairyland it is without its flower-decked locks.

Jerome K. Jerome, Three Men in a Boat

Hampton. Sudden snow in February adds magic to a marina above,
and to the parish church of Saint Mary, with the Pink Floyd's houseboat "Astoria" moored below

Hampton. A winter sunrise, left, and a summer sunset above, both seen from the photographer's base on Taggs Island

Hampton Court.
A flotilla, with crews
in period costumes,
celebrates the 500th
anniversary of the
accession of Henry VIII
to the English throne

Hampton Court. The Palace adds an extra glow to the moonlight, as skaters enjoy the winter ice rink

Richmond. Rowing boats heading home, below Richmond Bridge

Richmond. Young people gather at sunset on the Richmond riverfront…

Richmond. ...not always possible during Spring tides, when much of this stretch is under water

One man I knew had a very sad accident happen to him the first

time he went punting. He had been getting on so well that he

had grown quite cheeky over the business, and was walking up

and down the punt, working his pole with a grace that was quite

fascinating to watch. Oh, it was grand.

And it would have gone on being grand if he had not unfortunately,

while looking round to enjoy the scenery, taken just one more step

than there was any necessity for, and walked off the punt altogether.

The pole was firmly fixed in the mud, and he was left clinging to it while

the punt drifted away. It was an undignified position for him. A rude boy

on the bank immediately yelled out to a lagging chum to "hurry up and

see a real monkey on a stick".

Jerome K. Jerome, Three Men in a Boat

Richmond. The Great River Race, when seen here from Richmond, used to run from Ham to Greenwich but now heads in the opposite direction

Mortlake. Rowing eights prepare for their staggered start at the annual Head of the River Race

Mortlake. A week later, these are the final moments of the Oxford and Cambridge Boat Race, followed by a flotilla of officials, press and supporters

Kew. Period town houses line the riverbank at Kew, while new architecture rises above Nine Elms, a mile further down-stream

Hammersmith. **Early morning fog shrouds a houseboat community below Hammersmith Bridge**

London. **For one short month these four stone horsemen appeared on the south bank of the Thames, below the headquarters of MI6**

London. They were created by the artist Jason deCaires Taylor and titled "The Rising Tide"

There is no more thrilling sensation I know than sailing. It comes

as near to flying as man has got to yet - except in dreams.

The wings of the rushing wind seem to be bearing you onwards,

you know not where. You are no longer the slow, plodding, puny

thing of clay, creeping tortuously upon the ground; you are part

of Nature! Your heart is throbbing against hers. Her glorious

arms are around you, raising you up against her heart! Your

spirit is at one with hers; your limbs grow light! The voices of

the air are singing to you. The earth seems far away and little;

and the clouds so close above your head, are brothers, and you

stretch your arms to them.

Jerome K. Jerome, Three Men in a Boat

London. The Houses of Parliament, seen from Vauxhall Bridge

London. The Tattersall Castle is a floating pub and restaurant moored at the Embankment, after a former life as a ferry on the River Humber in the 1930s

London.
The Massey Shaw, a London Fire Brigade
fireboat before being restored by
enthusiasts, demonstrates the power of her
water cannon at Westminster

London. Oarsmen strain beneath Tower Bridge during the London Barge Match, which starts in Greenwich and ends at Westminster

I do not wish to be insulting, but I firmly believe that if you took an

average tow-line, and stretched it out across the middle of a field, and then

turned your back on it for thirty seconds, that, when you looked round

again, you would find that it had got itself altogether in a heap in the

middle of the field, and had twisted itself up, and tied itself into knots, and

lost its two ends, and become all loops; and it would take you a good half

hour, sitting down there on the grass and swearing all the while, to

disentangle it again.

This is my opinion of tow-lines in general. Of course, there may be

honourable exceptions; I do not say that there are not. There may be

tow-lines that are a credit to their profession - conscientious, respectable

tow-lines - tow-lines that do not imagine that they are crochet-work, and try

to knit themselves up into antimacassars the instant they are left to

themselves. I say there may be such tow-lines. I sincerely hope there are.

But I have not met with them.

Jerome K. Jerome, Three Men in a Boat

London. The Millennium Bridge, above, and Waterloo Bridge, right, seen towards sunset from the dome of Saint Paul's Cathedral

London. **Two hundred years after the death of Lord Nelson this funeral barge honours him during a river parade from Greenwich to Whitehall**

London. The warship HMS Belfast, with more firepower than Nelson could ever muster, salutes the great admiral's passing parade

London. A 130 metre long model of 17th century London prepares to meet a fiery end during a recreation of the
Great Fire of London on its 350th anniversary. The finely detailed structure was created by the American artist David Best

London. **Hours later, the Great Fire of London burns briefly once again, but this time with no casualties**

London. Musicians playing beneath Southwark's Globe Theatre and a street parade mark October Plenty, an annual Autumn Harvest celebration

London.
The Millennium Bridge, seen here from Tate
Modern, glides across the Thames towards
Saint Paul's Cathedral

197

London. **Girl with a Dolphin**, a sculpture by David Wynne, cavorts below Tower Bridge

London.
Fireworks bring an end to the Mayor of London's month long Thames Festival in September

London. A photo-call for members of the Marine Band of the Royal Netherlands attending the Classic Boat Festival at Saint Catherine's Dock

London. The Royal Nore, often used by the Queen on Thames journeys, takes her final voyage from Tower Pier to Gravesend. Over a sandwich lunch on-board, the Port of London Authority's Chairman, Christopher Rodrigues, signs her over as a gift to the Royal Yacht Britannia Trust's Rear Admiral Neil Rankin

Greenwich. Two sailing ships, the TS Rupel from Belgium and the Queen Galadriel from Denmark, pass below Canary Wharf during the Tall Ships Festival. Above, a jaunty sculpture of Lord Nelson looks on from a Greenwich pub.

Canary Wharf. Sunset and moon-glow illuminate London's financial centre, rising from the Isle of Dogs

Canary Wharf. A ferry leaves Canary Wharf towards that other financial centre, the City of London

Woolwich. The Thames Barrier, left, was built to protect London from flooding by the tidal Thames.
Above, a freighter loads sugar at the nearby Tate and Lyle plant

Tilbury. A Thames barge competing in the Greenwich to Gravesend Barge Match passes the container port of Tilbury

Gravesend.
Supporters follow the leaders of the barge race as they approach the Port of London Authority's pier at the end of the event

Near Southend. The skipper of the Thames barge "Adieu" ducks down to see past his sails during the annual Thames Sailing Barge Match

Near Southend.
Barges under full sail during the 73rd annual Thames Sailing Barge Match

Cover, Greenwich to Westminster Barge Race
Frontispiece, Fog below Hampton Court Palace
Back cover, Thames pub signs in East London
Above, Detail at Royal Naval College, Greenwich